WORLD WAR II CHRONICLES

EUROPE IN FLAMES

DWIGHT JON ZIMMERMAN,
MILITARY HISTORY CONSULTANT

BY JULIE KLAM

Published by Smart Apple Media, 1980 Lookout Drive, North Mankato, Minnesota 56003

Produced by Byron Preiss Visual Publications, Inc.

Library of Congress Cataloging-in-Publication Data

Klam, Julie.

Europe in flames/ by Julie Klam.

v. cm. — (World War II chronicles; bk. 1)

Summary: Describes the events in Europe leading up to World War II, relations between various European nations,
and specific battles and campaigns during the war.

ISBN 1-58340-187-3

1. World War, 1939-1945—Europe—Juvenile literature. 2. Europe—History—1918-1945—Juvenile literature.

[1. World War, 1939-1945—Europe. 2. Europe—History—1918-1945.] I. Title.

D743.7 .K53 2002

940.5—dc21   2002017700

First Edition

2 4 6 8 9 7 5 3 1

CONTENTS:

INTRODUCTION

✝ (opposite): Adolf Hitler addresses the Reichstag.

World War II was the greatest conflict of the 20th century. Fought on every continent except Antarctica and across every ocean, it was truly a "world war." Like many other wars, over time it evolved. Modern technology and strategic advancements changed the rules of combat forever, allowing for widespread attacks from the air, the ground, and the sea.

For the Chinese, the war began in 1931, when Japan invaded northeastern China. When Germany invaded Poland in 1939, Europeans were dragged into the fray. Americans did not enter World War II until December 7, 1941, when Japan attacked Pearl Harbor, Hawaii.

World War II pitted two sides against each other, the Axis powers and the Allied countries. The main Axis nations were Germany, Japan, and Italy. The Axis powers were led by Chancellor Adolf Hitler, the head of the Nazi Party in Germany; Premier Benito Mussolini, the head of the Fascists in Italy; and Japan's Emperor Hirohito and the military government headed by Prime Minister Hideki Tojo. The Allies included Britain, France, the Soviet Union, China, and the United States. The leaders of the Allies were Britain's Prime

✝ Benito Mussolini

✝ Hirohito

Winston Churchill

Minister Winston Churchill, who had replaced Neville Chamberlain in 1940; General Charles de Gaulle of France; the Soviet Union's Marshal Josef Stalin; China's Generalissimo Chiang Kai-shek; and Franklin Delano Roosevelt, the president of the United States. The two sides clashed primarily in the Pacific Ocean and Asia, which Japan sought to control, and in the Atlantic Ocean, Europe, and North Africa, where Germany and Italy were trying to take over.

World War II finally ended in 1945, first in Europe on May 8, with Germany's total capitulation. Then on September 2, the Japanese signed the document for their unconditional surrender after the United States had dropped two atomic bombs on Japan. World War II left 50 million people dead and millions of others wounded, both physically and mentally.

The war encompassed the feats of extraordinary heroes and the worst villains imaginable, with thrilling triumphs and heartrending tragedies. Starting with the end of World War I in 1918 and the rise of Hitler, *Europe in Flames* documents the German invasion of Poland in 1939, of Western Europe in 1940, and of the Soviet Union in 1941.

Charles de Gaulle

⊬ Josef Stalin

⊬ Chiang Kai-shek

⊬ (right): Franklin Delano Roosevelt

Map of German Conquests

- Germany (1939)
- Axis Occupied Territory (1942)
- Italy and Its Territories
- Treaty with Axis
- Allied Powers
- Allied Protectorates
- Neutral Countries
- Vichy France and Territories

NORWAY

SWEDEN

FINLAND

ESTONIA

North Sea

Baltic Sea

LATVIA

LITHUANIA

UNION OF SOVIET SOCIALIST REPUBLICS

IRELAND

UNITED KINGDOM

DENMARK

EAST PRUSSIA

THE NETHERLANDS

BELGIUM

GERMANY

POLAND

Atlantic Ocean

LUXEMBOURG

FRANCE

SLOVAKIA

SWITZERLAND

HUNGARY

VICHY FRANCE

ROMANIA

Black Sea

YUGOSLAVIA

PORTUGAL

SPAIN

ITALY

Adriatic Sea

BULGARIA

ALBANIA

TURKEY

GREECE

SYRIA

SPANISH MOROCCO

IRAQ

Mediterranean Sea

MOROCCO

PALESTINE

TRANS-JORDAN

ALGERIA

TUNISIA

EGYPT

SAUDI ARABIA

LIBYA

The Pacific Campaign

ALASKA

U.S.S.R.

ALEUTIAN ISLANDS

ATTU, KISKA
May-Aug. 1943

MONGOLIA

MANCHURIA

KOREA

JAPAN

CHINA

Doolittle Raid
Apr. 18, 1942

MIDWAY
June 1942

TIBET

OKINAWA
April-June 1945

IWO JIMA
Feb.- March 1945

PEARL HARBOR
Dec. 7, 1941

INDIA

BURMA

HONG KONG

THE PHILIPPINES
Oct. 1944-June 1945

SAIPAN, GUAM & TINIAN
June-Aug. 1944

FRENCH INDOCHINA

THAILAND

BORNEO

TARAWA
November 1943

DUTCH EAST INDIES

NEW GUINEA

AUSTRALIA

GUADALCANAL
Aug. 1942-Feb. 1943

U.S. aircraft carrier

Battle

Allied advance

Japanese possession
before Dec. 7, 1941

Japanese conquest
after Dec. 7, 1941

Limit of
Japanese expansion

Although the official start of World War II in Europe was Nazi Germany's invasion of Poland in September 1939, the seeds had been planted 20 years earlier at the end of World War I. Germany lost that war, but in many respects—especially in lives lost and property destroyed—the victors lost too.

Beginning in 1914, World War I pitted Great Britain, France, Russia, and Italy against Germany, Austria-Hungary, and the Ottoman Empire. At the beginning of World War I, the countries in the Ottoman Empire included Turkey, Syria, Lebanon, Palestine, Yemen, and parts of Saudi Arabia, Jordan, and Iraq. The Ottoman Empire was ruled by the Ottoman dynasty from its capital of Constantinople (modern-day Istanbul). The empire ruled the eastern Mediterranean from Greece to Egypt. Though the war was ignited by the assassination of Austria's Archduke Francis Ferdinand, the underlying fight was to determine who was to be the dominant world power in Europe—whose military was the strongest, whose status was the highest, and who had the most territory.

By the war's end in November of 1918, Russia had dropped out to deal with a civil war. The United States had entered with Italy, France, and Great Britain.

The Council of Four at the Versailles Peace Conference: (from left to right) British Prime Minister David Lloyd George, Italian Premier Vittorio Orlando, French Prime Minister Georges Clemenceau, and U.S. President Woodrow Wilson.

These nations, the Allies, won. The Allies now had to secure lasting peace. Their failure would ultimately cause the unrest that would become World War II.

The victors met at the Palace of Versailles near Paris in January 1919 to determine the terms of peace. The defeated countries were not invited. The Germans would be presented with the Treaty of Versailles in June 1919 for signature, not negotiation. Some of the things the treaty said were:

- The Germans would forfeit approximately 10 percent of their territory and population; some of the territory would be used to create Poland.
- Austria-Hungary and the Ottoman Empire would be cut into independent states.
- The French would occupy the German territory of the Rhineland and the Saar Basin, areas bordering France, for 15 years.
- Alsace and Lorraine, which France had lost to Germany in 1870, would be returned to France.
- All the German territories would be taken away from Germany and divided amongst the Allies.
- Germany would be disarmed—no tanks, no aircraft, no submarines—and only 100,000 ground troops would be allowed for internal security.
- Germany would be forced to take full responsibility for the war and pay the victors the total cost of the war, roughly $33 billion.

Needless to say, the Germans were not happy with the treaty, and by the early 1930s, the whole world would start to fear their wrath.

THE RISE OF HITLER

The post-World War I period was difficult for most of the world but particularly hard for the Germans. The Treaty of Versailles didn't leave them with much pride. In the 1920s, a war veteran with political ambitions named Adolf Hitler began to capitalize on people's attitudes. He began the Nazi, or National Socialist German Workers', Party. The Nazis believed that race was the most important trait in a country, and that their race, the Aryan race, defined primarily by non-Jewish Caucasians of Nordic decent, was superior to all others. In fact, they thought the Aryans were the master race and were put on earth to rule any "inferior," or non-Aryan, races.

In 1923, Hitler attempted a revolt against the German government. It landed him in jail, and it was there that he began dictating a best-selling autobiography and political testament, *Mein Kampf* (*My Struggle*). The book outlined and validated the German people's miseries and revealed Hitler's theories: that the Jews and the Communists were to blame for everything wrong and that a racially pure populace was paramount to the survival of Germany.

By the time he left prison, Hitler's reputation as a major political figure and incredibly persuasive public speaker had soared. He began lecturing about the inequity of the Treaty of Versailles and continued to blame the Jews for Germany's lowly position, calling them, among other things, "parasites." Promising to nullify the results of the war and restore Germany to greatness, Hitler emphasized the need to get Germany back the "living space" (*Lebensraum*) taken away from it in the Treaty of Versailles.

✛ (opposite): Hitler (behind podium in center) is sworn in as Chancellor of Germany, March 21, 1933.

After being appointed chancellor in 1933, Hitler wasted no time putting his plans in practice. He petitioned the League of Nations to begin rebuilding the German military. France vetoed the idea, and Germany withdrew from the League. Hitler then felt justified in expanding his remilitarization plan. He built a new Luftwaffe (air force) and instituted military conscription (both of which were illegal under the terms of the treaty). The League of Nations did not respond. In 1935, the British signed a pact allowing Germany to build a naval fleet approximately one-third the size of the British fleet, in effect nullifying the Treaty of Versailles.

Great Britain and France were concerned, but they refused to recognize the real danger. Hitler justified his actions to the world, saying he had been provoked by the injustice of the Treaty of Versailles. On March 7, 1936, Hitler ordered his troops to occupy the Rhineland (the German territory between the Rhine River and France, Belgium, Luxembourg, and the Netherlands), where he believed his people were suffering under foreign rule. Again, the League did nothing.

In 1938, Germany began an intense propaganda campaign to "unite" Austria with Germany. Hitler repeatedly referred to the *Anschluss,* or "union," of German-speaking people. He met with the chancellor of Austria and railed, "I have a historic mission and I am going to fulfill it because Providence has appointed me to do so!" An election was held to decide whether Austria should unite with Germany. After Hitler rigged the results in his favor, the Nazis marched into Austria and were hailed as heroes.

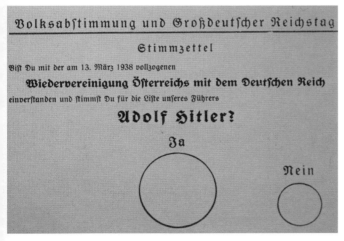

Volksabstimmung und Großdeutscher Reichstag

Stimmzettel

Bist Du mit der am 13. März 1938 vollzogenen

Wiedervereinigung Österreichs mit dem Deutschen Reich

einverstanden und stimmst Du für die Liste unseres Führers

Adolf Hitler?

Ja

Nein

✛ This ballot was used for the vote on the *Anschluss.*

THE RISE OF MUSSOLINI

While Hitler and the Nazi Party were securing control of Germany, Benito Mussolini and his Fascists were already in charge of Italy. Nazism and Fascism had a number of similarities, especially a belief in one-party dictatorship rule. In fact, Hitler was a big fan of Mussolini's, kept a picture of him on his desk, and emulated his methods to seize power. However, Nazism differed from Fascism in its extreme, fanatical belief in racial purity. Mussolini admitted that he couldn't get through *Mein Kampf* because it was too boring.

Mussolini was a big fan of military aggression. He felt conflict showed a nation's vitality. He also had a vision of creating a new Italian empire that rivaled the glory of Rome. His first conquest would be Ethiopia, an African nation that bordered the Italian possessions of Eritrea and Italian Somaliland. He saw Ethiopia as a stepping stone to the domination of Africa.

In October 1935, Italy invaded Ethiopia. With Italy's more than 330,000 men, poison gas, planes, and tanks, the small country led by Emperor Haile Selassie was no match. Selassie appealed to the League of Nations for assistance, and the League imposed some ineffectual economic sanctions on Italy. After a year, Italy took the Ethiopian capital of Addis Ababa, and Mussolini declared Ethiopia part of Italy's empire.

Mussolini addresses Fascist followers.

⊬ Abyssinian (Ethiopian) infantry, in 1936, fought the Italian army with outmoded weapons, including bows and arrows and spears.

Like Hitler, Mussolini stepped over the League of Nations to achieve his goal. The people of Ethiopia were brutalized and terrorized as the Fascists ruled their new colony.

THE MUNICH CONFERENCE

After securing Austria and the Rhineland, Hitler decided to use the same argument of "rescuing Germans under foreign rule" in Czechoslovakia, where three million ethnic Germans were under Czech rule. In the Sudetenland, an area of mountains that bordered Germany, Hitler claimed that Germans were being persecuted by the Czechs.

Czechoslovakia had a defense treaty with France and Great Britain. Therefore, Czechoslovakia refused to turn over the land to Germany, expecting France and Great Britain to honor their commitment and join Czechoslovakia in a war against Germany in the event of an attack.

The British prime minister, Neville Chamberlain, stepped in. He did not want war and believed that the issue could be decided in a friendly manner through discussions between Great Britain, France, Italy, and Germany.

On September 29, 1938, Mussolini, Hitler, Chamberlain, and Edouard Daladier, the French prime minister, met in Munich for a conference to figure out what should happen to Czechoslovakia. The Czechs were not invited. And neither were the Soviets, who had offered to help Czechoslavkia.

+ Neville Chamberlain

✛ Czech women greet German soldiers with the Nazi salute.

The outcome of the conference was predictable. Hitler would get what he wanted. France and Great Britain told Czechoslovakia to turn over the Sudetenland or fight the Germans alone. The Czechs had to give in, humiliated, angry, and betrayed.

In May 1939, Germany and Italy formed a formal alliance and called it the Pact of Steel. In it, both countries agreed to go to war in support of the other if either were attacked.

✛ (opposite): German tanks roll through a Sudeten street; the banner reads "Hail to Our German Brothers!"

THE OFFICIAL START OF WORLD WAR II

After Munich, France and Britain realized they should not have refused the Soviet Union's help with Czechoslovakia. In 1938, they opened the way for talks with the Soviet leader Josef Stalin. Stalin was a hard bargainer. Amongst other things, he wanted a guarantee that he could use Poland and Romania as bases in the event of a war. France and Britain wouldn't agree to this, but that was okay with Stalin. He was also bargaining with Hitler and had already planned to sign a treaty with Germany.

The German-Soviet Treaty of Nonaggression, also called the Hitler-Stalin Pact or the Nazi-Soviet Pact, was signed on August 23, 1939, in Moscow. The two countries agreed to trade machinery for food and other goods. In a secret provision of the treaty, Germany would let the Soviets occupy Latvia, Estonia, Lithuania, and Finland. Germany and the Soviet Union would divide Poland; and Germany would get a larger piece of Poland than the Soviets after the Germans invaded it. That decided, Hitler began to put his war plan in place. First he would conquer Poland, then France and Great Britain, and, later, he would fight the Soviets.

Again, France and Great Britain tried to step in diplomatically. The Treaty of Versailles had formed the Polish nation out of land taken from Germany, the Austria-Hungary Empire, and the Soviet Union.

⊬ Soviet Marshal Josef Stalin looks on as Soviet Foreign Minister Vyacheslav Mikhailovich Molotov signs the German-Soviet Treaty of Nonaggression, also known as the Hitler-Stalin Pact, with Germany on August 23, 1939.

Hitler pretended to negotiate, but on September 1, 1939, he declared war and invaded Poland.

On September 3, Great Britain and France declared war on Germany. But that declaration was too late to be of any help to the Poles. The Germans introduced a new kind of war: blitzkrieg, meaning "lightning war." The brave Polish troops were outmaneuvered and outnumbered. The German army and Luftwaffe defeated Poland in a way not seen before, quick and complete, utilizing a variety of tanks, aircraft, and weaponry. Modern advances and new technology granted more speed

✠ A German division advances into Poland in 1939.

⊦ A German Junkers Ju-87 "Stuka" dive-bomber

and firepower not available in World War I. With the blitzkrieg, German forces broke down not only the army under attack, but also its will to fight back.

Tens of thousands of troops surrendered to Germany. On September 17, the Soviet Union launched its own attack on the remaining Polish troops. By October 5, Poland had surrendered.

The Battle of the Atlantic, which began in 1939 between Great Britain and Germany, centered on Britain's attempt to stop the German navy, primarily its U-boats, from sinking British troop and supply ships. However, the first great clash in the Battle of the Atlantic took place not with U-boats but with the hunt for Germany's *Admiral Graf Spee*. The *Graf Spee* was a pocket battleship—fast, light, and heavily armed, a great threat to the Allied ships.

✠ The German battleship *Graf Spee* sinks off the coast of South America near Montevideo, Uruguay, December 17, 1939.

On December 13, 1939, the *Graf Spee* appeared near Uruguay. There it was surprised by three British cruisers, the *Exeter*, the *Ajax*, and the *Achilles*. For 14 hours, the ships pounded away at one another, then the *Graf Spee* left to find safe haven in the harbor at the capital of Uruguay, Montevideo. The neutral Uruguayans said the warship could stay for 72 hours before it had to leave. They ordered it out of their waters, and, after the captain and crew were removed on December 17, the *Graf Spee* scuttled, or blew itself up, at the mouth of the river Plate.

The captain, Hans Langsdorff, and his crew were interned in Uruguay. Three days later, Captain Langsdorff shot himself.

Two years after the victory over the *Graf Spee* in 1939, another dramatic sea battle took place in the Atlantic. The German battleship *Bismarck*, the fastest ship in the world at the time, left Poland and sailed through the British blockade. The powerful *Bismarck* posed a huge threat to British supply convoys.

After viewing the *Bismarck* in Norway on May 21, 1941, Britain began tracking it. On May 24, two British ships, the battle-cruiser *Hood* and the battleship *Prince of Wales*, began pummeling the *Bismarck*, which strongly defended itself. The *Hood* was sunk, and the *Prince of Wales* was hit and forced to disengage. But the *Bismarck* had suffered damage, too. It suffered additional damage when it was torpedoed by aircraft from the British carrier *Victorious*. Limping away, the German battleship leaked a trail of oil as it tried to seek shelter in occupied France.

On May 26, not yet having reached its destination, the *Bismarck* came under further British attack. British planes torpedoed it, and more ships surrounded and opened fire on it. Though unable to pierce the *Bismarck*'s armored deck, the British were able to destroy its turrets and force it to sink.

Though the British lost the *Hood* and suffered damage to other ships, the Germans had lost their greatest battleship. After enduring some discouraging setbacks on land, the British people needed a victory at sea to boost their waning morale.

✠ British Royal Navy Swordfish biplanes prepare to take off from a British aircraft carrier for an attack against the German battleship *Bismarck*, May 1941.

THE PHONY WAR

After Germany's invasion of Poland in 1939 came one of the strangest periods of World War II. The French army sat in the Maginot Line, a state-of-the-art alternative to the trenches of World War I with an elaborate underground complex of railroads, hospitals, command posts, supply depots, and barracks. At the same time, the Germans remained passive. The period between fall 1939 and winter 1940 was called the "Phony War," or *Sitzkrieg,* the German term meaning "sitting war."

During this interlude, opposing forces rested right in front of each other, outposts were quiet, and German supplies moved up the Rhine railroad undisturbed by the French. Hitler was not idle but was actually refitting his army from the Polish campaign and plotting future activities. The British and the French were hoping that Poland might be Hitler's only ambition and that they had been spared fighting. They would have no such luck.

✝ (opposite): A December 1944 photograph shows U.S. soldiers examining a Maginot Line fort near Climbach, France.

✝ A political cartoon depicts a "Nazi dove of peace" standing on a skull that represents the defeated Poland.

THE RUSSO-FINNISH WAR

Finland had once been part of the old imperial Russia, but it had succeeded in gaining independence after the Russian Revolution of 1917. After he had made the Hitler-Stalin Pact, Stalin decided he wanted the Finnish territory near Leningrad back and he wanted navy-port rights. The Finns declined to cede Russia this territory.

In November 1939, Stalin sent troops, and in one of its last feeble acts, the League of Nations expelled the Soviets from their organization. The Finns staged a heroic defense of their country. It was a David versus Goliath conflict that seized the world's imagination. Though the Finns were outnumbered by the Soviets, their knowledge of the terrain and their tenacity and tactical brilliance made them a worthy foe.

Again, the United States remained neutral, but it provided Finland with $30 million in aid. The British and French sent volunteers and small amounts of weapons and materials.

Ultimately, the Finns were overwhelmed and the Finnish Parliament accepted the terms of peace given by the Soviets. According to those terms, the Finns would remain independent but the Soviet border would be extended. The victory cost the Soviets 200,000 men, almost 700 planes, and 1,600 tanks—as well as humiliation before the court of world opinion.

THE GERMAN INVASION OF DENMARK AND NORWAY AND THE END OF CHAMBERLAIN

In order to keep building his war machine, Hitler needed to secure supplies of Swedish iron ore. He also had to protect Germany's access to food from Denmark and Norway. To ensure his supply, he decided to invade these countries next.

Denmark had no idea what was coming. On April 9, 1940, Hitler invaded and, after threatening to bomb, forced a surrender the very same day. Hitler simultaneously invaded Norway. Surprised as well, the Norwegians were able to hold off the Germans until the royal family escaped to London. Though they were outmatched, the Norwegian troops did not surrender.

On April 10, help arrived in the form of Allied troops from France and Great Britain. The British navy sank 10 German destroyers and 2 cruisers, half of their

✛ Germans invade Norway in April 1940.

entire surface navy. By the invasion's end, Germany's navy would be decimated, at least for some time.

The Germans had taken the Norwegian city of Narvik, which bordered Sweden in the North, unopposed. With the help of 25,000 Allied troops, the Norwegians took Narvik back. For a while it seemed that the Allies might win, but then in May, Germany attacked the Netherlands, Britain, and France.

When the Allies pulled out to aid the Netherlands and Belgium against the German offensive, the Norwegians were alone again and didn't have the strength to defend themselves. On June 9, they agreed to an armistice and 300,000 German soldiers were stationed in Norway, securing the supply route for Swedish iron ore.

Partially as a result of the Allied debacle in Scandinavia, Prime Minister Chamberlain began rapidly losing his already dwindling support in Britain. Defections plagued his party, and on May 10, 1940, he resigned.

Although he also bore some of the responsibility for the failures in Scandinavia, Winston Churchill, an outspoken voice and First Lord of the Admiralty, was the man Britain wanted to replace Chamberlain. Churchill had support from many Britons, who felt he had the charisma and presence to match Hitler. Chamberlain remained in Churchill's cabinet as Lord President of the Council, until illness forced him to resign in October 1940. He died of cancer the following month.

GERMANY INVADES THE NETHERLANDS, BELGIUM, AND LUXEMBOURG

In January 1940, Hitler had plans to invade the Netherlands, Belgium, and Luxembourg, but a breach of security coupled with bad weather caused him to change his plans and postpone his attack until spring. May 10, 1940, Churchill's first day on the job as prime minister, proved to be a weighty one. On that day, the Phony War, the period during which nothing happened, ended.

The Nazi blitzkrieg swept across the Netherlands, Belgium, and Luxembourg sometime after midnight. The Germans said they were protecting the territories from attacks by Great Britain and France, but they added that any resistance from the citizens of the regions would be pointless.

During the invasion of the Netherlands, the undefended city of Rotterdam was attacked by the Luftwaffe. Bombs from the German warplanes wrecked the city, killing hundreds of civilians and injuring thousands more. This style of warfare, mass bombing of cities, would eventually be used by both sides in the war.

Belgium had earlier declined Britain and France's offer to help defend it in the event of an attack; the Belgians had believed their neutrality would keep them out of the war. When the invasion came, Belgium had to wait while British and French troops advanced into place. While the Allies tried desperately to turn back the attack, King Leopold of Belgium surrendered on May 28.

THE BATTLE OF FRANCE

At the same time Hitler was attacking the Netherlands, Belgium, and Luxembourg, he was also moving in against France. Hitler directed his tanks to avoid the Maginot Line by passing north of it through the Ardennes Forest of Belgium. Tanks and infantry under the protection of Luftwaffe dive-bombers came through the Ardennes without opposition on May 10, 1940.

The attack stunned the Allies. Unlike in World War I, where the British and French troops had managed to rally and stop the German advance, now, 22 years later, the German invasion was overcoming all opposition.

Shortly after the campaign had begun, Churchill refused to allow any more RAF (Royal Air Force) squadrons to be deployed in France. He wanted to preserve them for Britain's homeland battles. This left the desperate leaders of France feeling abandoned and betrayed.

France made pleas to President Roosevelt for help, asking him to send "a cloud of planes." Roosevelt said he didn't have them.

By June 22, 1940, the Battle of France was over. In the same railroad car used to sign the surrender documents of World War I, France formally surrendered to Germany.

Hitler wasted no time exacting revenge for the Treaty of Versailles. There were no negotiations; the French were forced to agree. They would formally surrender at Compiègne, a town north of Paris. The Germans would occupy northern and western France. The French army would be reduced to 100,000 and the navy would be demilitarized. Hitler decided not to occupy all of France to avoid further

France surrenders to Germany at Compiègne, June 22, 1940, inside the same railroad car the Germans had surrendered to the Allies in at the end of World War I.

French resistance. He also charged the French millions of dollars in reparations to pay for the cost of the occupation.

The Germans also allowed the French to set up a collaborationist government, led by Henri Philippe Pétain, a hero of World War I, under their watchful eye, in the spa town of Vichy. This German-friendly government contrasted with the small group of Frenchmen led by General Charles de Gaulle who refused to accept France's defeat. They organized a "Free French" government-in-exile, which fought on the side of the Allies.

ISOLATIONISM AND NEUTRALITY IN THE UNITED STATES

Prior to WWII, isolationism had a long and important history in America, beginning with President George Washington's admonishing the nation to keep out of "foreign entanglements." Subsequently, under President Monroe, the Monroe Doctrine audaciously stated that Europe should stay out of the Americas, and if it did not, the United States would defend the hemisphere.

Congress passed Neutrality Acts in 1935, 1936, and 1937, making U.S. involvement with nations fighting in World War II virtually impossible through bans on loans and military actions. In addition, the United States had also pared down its military and defense spending after World War I.

Though the U.S. Congress had shed its isolationist sentiments in 1917 and agreed to declare war on the Central Powers in WWI, it rejected membership in the League of Nations, which was created after the war's end. So with war clouds forming in Europe and Asia, the isolationists, who prior to December 7, 1941, were the majority of the population, did everything they could to keep America out of the war.

✈ An American tank, part of a Lend-Lease shipment, is assembled after arriving in England.

At the point in the Battle of France when that country was desperately looking for help from America, the U.S. Army included only 160,000 men and was ranked 16th in the world. One of America's key weaknesses was the near total absence of an air force. While armies in Europe were building themselves up more than ever before, President Roosevelt kept the military defense budget at a minimum through the late 1930s. His defenders say the isolationists had his hands tied and he could do nothing, but others complain that he never appealed to the American people and let them know what was at stake.

Despite the Neutrality Acts, Roosevelt had managed to keep Britain supplied with aid, but the cost of fighting a war was so high that very soon Britain would no longer be able to pay for all the things they needed.

Sensing that popular opinion was turning against isolationism, in 1941 Roosevelt asked Congress to pass a measure that he said would help the United States stay out of the war while providing aid to the Allies. In one of his famous Fireside Chats, Roosevelt used the imagery of a "helping neighbor" story—of a man whose house was on fire and a neighbor who loaned him his garden hose to help put out the fire. The man with the burning house was Great Britain. The man with the hose was America. Roosevelt proposed a Lend-Lease agreement—America would lend Great Britain certain war materials (in this case, 50-year-old destroyers) in exchange for long-term military-base leases on strategic islands. This was the start of the Lend-Lease agreement.

✚ English women carry American rifles delivered as part of the Lend-Lease agreement.

DUNKIRK

One of the most amazing moments in British history took place in 1940 in Dunkirk, a French port on the English Channel not too far away from the Belgian border. Allied troops in Belgium had been cut off and surrounded on three sides during the German invasion of France. With their backs to the sea, the British commander, Field Marshal Lord Gort, decided that the best move would be to evacuate as many troops as possible through Dunkirk. Churchill agreed and gave the order to launch the plan called Operation Dynamo. It was hoped as many as 45,000 men would be rescued.

The Royal Navy began to call to service every ship and boat that could be located along the south of Britain. The evacuation of Dunkirk began on May 26, 1940. The RAF brilliantly battled the German Luftwaffe, who were staging constant bombing raids on the site of embarkation in an attempt to single-handedly stop the rescue.

Despite the fact that they were forced to abandon all their heavy weaponry, from the first evacuations until their completion nine days later, it was estimated that 338,226 Allied soldiers were rescued from Dunkirk. More than 800 vessels, from battleships to private fishing boats, contributed to the evacuation. In their nine days of bombing, the Germans succeeded in sinking only 6 destroyers, 8 personnel ships, and approximately 200 small craft.

✠ British troops are rescued during the evacuation at Dunkirk, France, in May 1940.

ITALY VERSUS ENGLAND IN NORTH AFRICA

During World War II, most countries in Africa were territories under the control of different European nations. The Italians decided after the fall of France that they had to protect their territories in northern Africa from the Allies. Their possessions extended from Libya to the Horn of Africa (Italian Somaliland, Ethiopia, and Eritrea). Mixed into these areas were some British possessions, including Egypt, the Sudan, and British Somaliland. Within these countries lay the key to northern Africa: the Suez Canal, located in Egypt.

Mussolini assumed the best time to drive the British out of Africa was when, following France's defeat in June 1940, their homeland was being attacked by the Germans in the Battle of Britain.

By July 1940, Italian troops in Ethiopia captured an outpost on the Kenya border, and crossed into the Sudan. In August, they invaded British Somaliland. In September, their planes attacked from Libya, and Italian troops occupied a position 60 miles (97 km) from the Egyptian border.

In February 1941, Indian and South African units, along with a number of other British-African units, rallied. They captured Mogadishu, the capital of Italian Somaliland, and chased the Italian troops out of Kenya. In March, they had liberated British Somaliland. By April, they also had liberated Addis Ababa, the capital of Ethiopia. Further north, a year later, they drove the Italians back 5,000 miles (8,047 km) through Libya, capturing 130,000 prisoners.

In the African campaign, the Italians lost almost 300,000 men, most of whom surrendered.

＋ British troops advance over the North African desert toward the Axis-held town of Benghazi, Libya, September 1940.

ITALY ATTACKS ALBANIA AND GREECE

In 1939, Mussolini had the Italian army invade Albania, a small nation facing Italy across the Adriatic Sea, which was quickly overrun. By the fall of 1940, Mussolini was jealous of all of Germany's conquests and decided to win something big for Italy. Mussolini next set his eyes on Greece, thinking that it would be another easy conquest. On October 28, 1940, his armies attacked. But instead of collapsing, the Greeks fought back with skill and determination. The Italian invasion was driven back into Albania with humiliating losses.

In April 1941, Hitler was forced to come to the aid of the Italians. This meant that he had to delay Operation Barbarossa, his planned invasion of the Soviet Union. But he couldn't let Mussolini be defeated. He gave the orders to transfer troops for the invasion of Greece.

✛ Greek soldiers guard a mountain pass in Albania against Italian army attack.

GERMANY INVADES YUGOSLAVIA AND GREECE

 A German Panzer unit moves into Salonika, Greece, during the Balkan campaign of 1941.

Hitler feared that the Allies' success in Greece could cause Germany major damage. Also, as a matter of pride, he could not allow his fellow dictator to be defeated. If left to their own devices, the Allies would be able to build air bases in Greece and, in turn, attack Hitler's oil source in Romania and threaten other German resources.

Hitler was in good position to stage the attack on Greece. His neighboring countries of Romania, Hungary, and Bulgaria were all Axis nations, allowing the Germans easy access to Greece. But the Germans needed one other country to join them: Yugoslavia.

The Yugoslavian government reluctantly agreed to join the Axis, but in March 1941, rebels overthrew the government and, in essence, tore up the Axis treaty. Yugoslavia received no help from the Soviet Union because Stalin didn't want to anger Hitler. And though the Yugoslav army contained almost one million men, there was so much fighting between the ethnic Serbs and the Croats, that they couldn't unify to rally against the Germans.

On April 6, 1941, the Germans began their trademark air attack, followed by ground troops and tanks. Eleven days later, Yugoslavia surrendered. But many Yugoslav soldiers escaped through the woods of Yugoslavia and joined the partisans, one strong and successful resistance group that was headed by Josip Broz, known by his code name Tito.

At the same time, the Germans also entered Greece to aid the Italians. About a half million German troops were involved in the invasion. By the middle of June, Greece and its islands had been conquered. But Operation Barbarossa had been critically delayed.

The U-boats, German submarines, were the scourge of the high seas. After 1941, U-boats moved in "Wolf Packs," in which, like wolves, they grouped together to attack the weakest and slowest ships.

The war against the U-boats was the longest-running engagement in the Battle of the Atlantic. Britain, who had begun to receive real support from the technically neutral United States, was determined to keep shipping and supply lanes open against the brutal and expert U-boats.

In a move that was barely short of entering the war, Roosevelt sent naval units for convoy duty. He and Churchill divided up the Atlantic, with the United States taking the area west of Iceland. The U.S. Navy escorted the British convoys, and on September 4, 1940—more than a year before America officially went to war—the USS *Greer* fought a battle with a German U-boat. Neither ship was harmed, but the incident caused Roosevelt to issue an order to the navy to shoot German warships on sight. In mid-October 1941, the USS *Kearny* was torpedoed but didn't sink; on October 31, the

This Atlantic convoy, as seen from one of the warships, is assigned to guard the transport ships.

destroyer USS *Reuben James* was not so lucky. Hit by just one torpedo, it exploded, blown in two, and 115 Americans were lost.

After the fall of France, Germany ruled the Atlantic. With 2,500 miles (4,023 km) of coastline occupied by Germany, Hitler had all the room he needed to launch his U-boats. British destroyers were keeping close to home because of the threat of an invasion of Britain by Germany. Between July and October 1940, each U-boat sank an average of eight Allied ships per month; German submariners understandably referred to this period as the "Happy Time."

But by the following summer, the threat of invasion had passed, and British defense had improved, especially in code breaking. The British Admiralty was now able to decipher the orders German Admiral Karl Doenitz gave to his captains. This ability gave the British a huge advantage on the sea. Unfortunately, it would take many months—and the entry of the United States into the war—before the Allies would win the Battle of the Atlantic.

✝ The German World War II code machine, "Enigma"

BARBAROSSA

By the spring of 1941, Hitler was in the midst of a blistering winning streak. For his next and largest conquest, he chose the Soviet Union, in a plan called Operation Barbarossa. Stalin's intelligence picked up numerous pieces of information, confirmed by Allied intelligence, that the advance would take place. But Stalin would not believe it, and when the Germans struck at 4:15 A.M. on June 22, 1941, the Soviets were wholly unprepared.

More than 3.5 million German soldiers, 3,600 tanks, 13 motorized divisions, 7,000 weapons, and 2,500 aircraft were involved in the attack. Also, the German allies Italy, Romania, Hungary, and Bulgaria supplied 1.3 million additional men. The Soviet Red Army included more than two million men, but because of Stalin's refusal to alert the defenses, the Soviet high command was ill-prepared to fight.

The German military was miles behind the front lines by the time the Soviets realized what was happening. Orders were frantically dispatched to the troops, but they were made irrelevant by the speed of the invaders' assault. Britain and the United States pledged to give the Soviets their support.

By August, the Germans had enveloped and captured Soviet army after Soviet army, destroyed squadrons of airplanes, captured thousands of weapons and tanks, and seized hundreds of miles of territory. Another German victory seemed inevitable and imminent. The Russians, Belorussians, Ukranians, and other Slavic people were initially all too willing to help the Germans. They hated the harsh Soviet rule and Stalin's assorted programs. But because Hitler regarded the

⊬ A German He-111 bomber drops bombs on a target in the Russian front.

Slavs as *Untermenschen*, a lower racial order, he wanted them eradicated. Thus Hitler's prejudice wound up hurting him in a key way. Instead of making the locals allies, his policies turned them into partisans. The Germans' attack drove deep into the Soviet Union. Hundreds of thousands of Soviet troops were captured. In the fall, after some indecision, Hitler ordered that the German army's main goal should be the capture of Moscow.

The Germans' drive to Moscow continued into December 1941. The Soviets were beaten down but were about to receive help from another ally who would prove to be unbeatable: the Russian winter.

With temperatures reaching -30 °F (-34 °C), German aircraft was grounded. Hitler's men suffered from exposure, tank and truck engines wouldn't start, and weapons wouldn't fire. A final effort from Siberian soldiers, reinforcements that had been held in reserve for this moment, forced the Germans, within sight of Moscow, to retreat for the first time in World War II.

Hitler was enraged. He saw that many of his generals were panicking. He promptly ordered the retreating forces to stop, turn around, and fight to the last man. He also replaced generals left and right. From this point on, Hitler began to personally direct the battle, and would continue to do so for the rest of the war not only in the east, but in other areas as well. The Soviets did eventually prevail with a good deal of help from the United States, who extended Lend-Lease aid to them on June 24, 1941, two days after the Soviet Union was invaded.

Less than six months later, the United States would officially enter the war as a result of the Japanese attack on Pearl Harbor on December 7, 1941.

GLOSSARY

Allies—The name for the nations, primarily Great Britain, the United States, the Soviet Union, and France, united against the Axis powers.

Axis—The countries, primarily Germany, Italy, and Japan, that fought against the Allies.

Blitzkrieg—The German word for "lightning war." A swift, overpowering military offensive of combined land and air forces led by tanks or other armored vehicles.

Campaign—A series of major military operations designed to achieve a long-range goal.

Capitulation—An agreement of surrender.

Fascism—A philosophy or system of government that advocates dictatorship and extreme nationalism.

Fireside Chats—The informal name for President Franklin Roosevelt's radio speeches to the American people that updated them on important events of the day.

Isolationists—Those who advocate that their country remain aloof from political or economic relationships with other countries, especially ones at war.

League of Nations—A world organization of nations established in 1920 for the purpose of peacefully promoting diplomatic relations and commerce. It was dissolved in 1946 and replaced by the United Nations.

Luftwaffe—The German Air Force.

Maginot Line—A series of interlocking fortifications composed of minefields, artillery and machine-gun bunkers, and other defenses constructed on the French border with Germany.

Mein Kampf—In English, "My Struggle"; Adolph Hitler's book that was both his autobiography and a statement of his political beliefs and plans.

Nazi—The acronym for NAtionalsoZIalist, the first word of the official title of Hitler's political party, the Nationalsozialistische Deutsche Arbeiterpartie or NSDAP (National Socialist German Workers' Party).

Pocket battleship—A term for Germany's supposedly smaller and less powerful battleships.

Resistance—An underground organization engaged in the struggle for national liberation in a country under military occupation.

Soviet Union—From 1917–1991, the nation known officially as the Union of Soviet Socialist Republics; a nation containing 15 communist-governed republics and dominated by its largest republic, Russia.

INDEX

Abyssinia. *See* Ethiopia
Addis Ababa
 Italian invasion of, 16
 liberation of, 39
Africa, 6, 39, 41
Albania, Italian invasion, 40
Allied powers, 4–6, 31–32, 33, 34–35
 evacuation at Dunkirk, 38
 in World War I, 10–12
Anschluss, of Austria with Germany, 15
Aryan race, 13
Asia, 6, 36
Atlantic Ocean, 6
 Battle of, 26–27, 42
Atomic bombs, 6
Austria, union of Germany with, 15
Austria-Hungary, 10–12, 22
Axis powers, 4–6
 and German invasion of Belgium, 32–34, 38
Bismarck, 26–27
Blitzkrieg, 24–25, 33
British Navy
 in Battle of the Atlantic, 26–27
 and German invasion of Denmark and Norway, 31–32
Chamberlain, Neville, 6, 19, 32
Chiang Kai-shek, 6–7
Churchill, Winston S., 6, 34, 42
 as British prime minister, 32, 33
Communists, Nazi Party versus, 13
Council of Four, 10–11
Czechoslovakia, 19–21
de Gaulle, Charles, 6, 35
Denmark, 31–32
Dunkirk, Allied evacuation

from, 38
"Enigma" code machine, 43
Estonia, 22
Ethiopia, 16–18, 39
Europe 4, 6
 American isolationism and, 36–37
 in World War I, 10–12
Fascism, 4, 16–18
Finland, Soviet occupation of, 22, 30
Fireside Chats, 37
France, 4–6, 30, 31–32, 33
 American isolationism and, 37
 declaration of war against Germany, 24
 German annexation of Sudetenland, 19–21
 German-Soviet Nonaggression Treaty and, 22
 in Phony War, 28–29
 and post-World War I Germany, 15
 surrender of, 34–35
 in World War I, 10–12
"Free French" government-in-exile, 35
Germany, 4, 6
 annexation of Sudetenland by, 19–21
 in Battle of the Atlantic, 26–27
 conquests by (map), 8
 creation of Poland from, 22
 evacuation at Dunkirk, 38
 German-Soviet Nonaggression Treaty and, 22–25
 invasion of Denmark and Norway, 31–32
 invasion of France by,

34–35
 invasion of Greece by, 41
 invasion of Netherlands, Belgium, and Luxembourg by, 33
 invasion of Soviet Union by, 44–45
 invasion of Yugoslavia by, 41
 Pact of Steel with Italy, 21
 in Phony War, 28
 after Treaty of Versailles, 13–15
 U-boats of, 42–43
 in World War I, 10–12
Graf Spee, 26
Great Britain, 4–6, 31–32, 33
 in Battle of the Atlantic, 26–27, 42
 declaration of war against Germany, 24
 German annexation of Sudetenland and, 19–21
 German-Soviet Nonaggression Treaty and, 22
 Lend-Lease agreements with, 36–37
 Operation Barbarossa and, 44
 and post-World War I Germany, 15
 Russo-Finnish War and, 30
 U-boats and, 42–43
 versus Italy in North Africa, 10–12, 39
Greece, 41
Hitler, Adolf, 4–5, 31, 33, 34–35, 40, 41
 Operation Barbarossa and, 44–45
 in Phony War, 28
 Poland invaded by, 22–25